Contents

Introduction

The *Spelling for Literacy* series is well established as the leading spelling resource in use in schools across the United Kingdom. Now fully updated to meet the demands of the new National Curriculum, teachers can feel confident that each book covers all the spellings required for their year group.

This is the fifth book in the series, covering spellings suitable for Year 5 arising from the word patterns, suffixes and prefixes that are specified as statutory requirements for Years 5 and 6. All the non-statutory example words listed in the National Curriculum are also included, together with other words that follow similar patterns.

As stated in the National Curriculum, Year 5 and Year 6 pupils should be reminded of the work they have learnt in previous years. They learn the use of a wide range of word endings as well as of 'silent' letters. They also learn a range of homophones and other words that are often confused.

In a working environment of praise and enjoyment, the activities contained in this book will provide ample opportunities for meeting the statutory requirements as shown below.

Work for Year 5 and 6

STATUTORY REQUIREMENTS

- Endings which sound like /ʃəəs/ spelt –cious or –tious
- Endings which sound like /ʃəəl/
- Words ending in –ant, –ance/–ancy, –ent, –ence/–ency
- Words ending in –able and –ible
- Words ending in –ably and –ibly
- Adding suffixes beginning with vowel letters to words ending in –fer

- Use of the hyphen
- Words with the /iː/ sound spelt ei after c
- Words containing the letter-string ough
- Words with 'silent' letters (i.e. letters whose presence cannot be predicted from the
- pronunciation of the word)
- Homophones and other words that are often confused

Suggestions for using this book...

The words are arranged in sets, usually of ten words but in some cases twelve or sixteen. Each set of words is used in three styles of sheet:

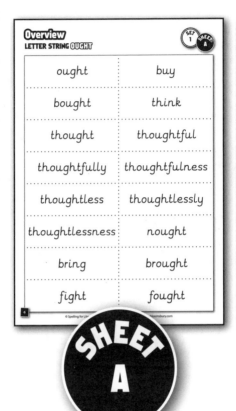

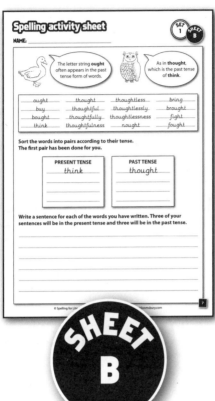

Overview

- Can be displayed on-screen for discussion.

- Can be printed out and displayed as 'Words of the Week'.

Spelling activity sheet

- To be used as part of a lesson.

- A perfect follow-up activity for the learning that has taken place using Sheet A and ideal for homework.

Learn, write, check

- Children look at the words, say them out loud and write them down, before covering the first two columns, re-writing the words and then checking them.

- Can be used in class.

- Can be used as homework.

ought	buy
bought	think
thought	thoughtful
thoughtfully	thoughtfulness
thoughtless	thoughtlessly
thoughtlessness	nought
bring	brought
fight	fought

Spelling activity sheet

NAME: _____

The letter string **ought** often appears in the past tense form of words.

As in **thought**, which is the past tense of **think**.

ought	thought	thoughtless	bring
buy	thoughtful	thoughtlessly	brought
bought	thoughtfully	thoughtlessness	fight
think	thoughtfulness	nought	fought

Sort the words into pairs according to their tense.
The first pair has been done for you.

PRESENT TENSE

think

_____

_____

_____

PAST TENSE

thought

_____

_____

_____

Write a sentence for each of the words you have written. Three of your sentences will be in the present tense and three will be in the past tense.

_____

_____

_____

_____

_____

Learn, write, check

NAME: _____

Look and say	Write then cover	Write then check
ought		
buy		
bought		
think		
thought		
thoughtful		
thoughtfully		
thoughtfulness		
thoughtless		
thoughtlessly		
thoughtlessness		
nought		
bring		
brought		
fight		
fought		

tough	toughen
enough	cough
though	although
dough	through
thorough	thoroughly
borough	plough
bough	rough
roughen	roughly

NAME: _____

The letters **ough** can make several different sounds.

Like **uff**, **off**, **oo**, **o**, **u** and **ow**.

tough	cough	through	plough	roughly
toughen	though	thorough	bough	thought
enough	although	thoroughly	rough	
thoughtful	dough	borough	roughen	

Sort the words according to the sounds made by ough.

ow _____

_____

_____

off _____

_____

oo _____

_____

uff _____

_____

_____

_____

_____

o _____

_____

_____

u _____

_____

_____

or _____

_____

Write the correct words to fill the gaps in the sentences.

The teacher _____ that we _____ deserved our rewards.

I had to take some medicine for my _____.

The road was very _____ so it was hard to ride my bike.

The dog jumped _____ a hole in the fence.

The farmer made the _____ go in a straight line.

You have to knead the _____ before making the bread.

NAME: _____

Look and say	Write then cover	Write then check
tough		
toughen		
enough		
cough		
though		
although		
dough		
through		
thorough		
thoroughly		
borough		
plough		
bough		
rough		
roughen		
roughly		

possible	possibly
impossible	impossibly
horrible	horribly
terrible	terribly
visible	visibly
incredible	incredibly
sensible	sensibly
probable	probably

Spelling activity sheet

NAME: _____

The word **sensible** is related to the root word **sense**.

But there isn't a root word for **possible**.

possible	horrible	visible	sensible
possibly	horribly	visibly	sensibly
impossible	terrible	incredible	probable
impossibly	terribly	incredibly	probably

When the words 'possible' and 'possibly' are put in alphabetical order, 'possible' has to come first because e comes before y.

Write all the words in alphabetical order. The first word will be 'horrible' and the last word will be 'visibly'.

_____ _____ _____ _____

_____ _____ _____ _____

_____ _____ _____ _____

_____ _____ _____ _____

Look at this word: *possibility*

Find four more words that end in 'bility'.

_____ _____ _____ _____

13

Learn, write, check

NAME: _____

Look and say	Write then cover	Write then check
possible		
possibly		
impossible		
impossibly		
horrible		
horribly		
terrible		
terribly		
visible		
visibly		
incredible		
incredibly		
sensible		
sensibly		
probable		
probably		

adore	adorable
adorably	adoration
apply	applicable
applicably	application
consider	considerable
considerably	consideration
tolerate	tolerable
tolerably	toleration

Spelling activity sheet

NAME: _____

 We've seen words that end with **ible**.

 Even more words end with **able**.

adore	applicable	adorable
tolerate	consideration	considerable
adoration	applicably	tolerable
considerably	toleration	adorably
apply	application	
tolerably	consider	

Write the words in sets. One set is done for you.

adore	_____	_____	_____
adorable	_____	_____	_____
adorably	_____	_____	_____
adoration	_____	_____	_____

Write a set of words for each root word. You may need to think beyond the suffixes used on this page!

remove _____ _____ _____

restore _____ _____ _____

Learn, write, check

NAME: _____

Look and say	Write then cover	Write then check
adore		
adorable		
adorably		
adoration		
apply		
applicable		
applicably		
application		
consider		
considerable		
considerably		
consideration		
tolerate		
tolerable		
tolerably		
toleration		

banana	camera
umbrella	koala
tarantula	sofa
area	gala
puma	pizza
samba	sauna
siesta	fiesta
bacteria	paella

Spelling activity sheet

NAME: _____

Thousands of words end in **e**.

Not very many end with an **a**.

Look at these words that end in a. Sort them into four lists.
Remember that names of places must begin with a capital letter.

koala	Asia	paella	samba	Africa
camera	puma	umbrella	pizza	fiesta
sauna	siesta	tarantula	bacteria	banana
America	gala	Alabama	sofa	gorilla

Write a set of words for each root word.

FOOD	PLACES	CREATURES	OTHER WORDS

Draw and label a picture of one of the following:

1. A tarantula eating a banana.

2. A koala sitting on a sofa eating a pizza.

3. A puma having a siesta under an umbrella.

4. A gorilla with a camera eating paella.

Learn, write, check

NAME: _____

Look and say	Write then cover	Write then check
banana		
camera		
umbrella		
koala		
tarantula		
sofa		
area		
gala		
puma		
pizza		
samba		
sauna		
siesta		
fiesta		
bacteria		
paella		

kangaroo	potato
tomato	risotto
flamingo	mango
armadillo	volcano
echo	cuckoo
radio	piano
cello	banjo
igloo	tattoo

Spelling activity sheet

NAME: _____

Some of the plurals of these words have an **e** before the **s**.

Potato becomes **potatoes** and **echo** becomes **echoes**.

cuckoo	potato	cello	volcano
piano	banjo	mango	kangaroo
echo	risotto	tomato	radio
armadillo	tattoo	igloo	flamingo

Use the words to solve the clues. Some clues are pictures and some are words.

1 Australian leaping animal. _____

2 Reflection of sound waves causes this. _____

3 An orchestral stringed instrument. _____

4 An icy home. _____

5 An Italian rice dish. _____

6 Armour-clad South American creature. _____

7 This can be used to make chips. _____

8 Skin decoration. _____

9 Bright red fruit eaten in salad. _____

10 Golden tropical fruit. _____

11 This bird lays eggs in other birds' nests. _____

12 Tall long-necked bird. _____

13  _____

14  _____

15 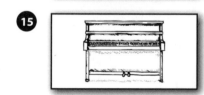 _____

16 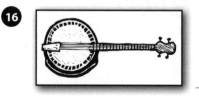 _____

Work with a friend and make a list of all the words you can find that end in o. Now use a dictionary to help you to find out how to write the plural of each of your words.

Learn, write, check

NAME: _____

Look and say	Write then cover	Write then check
kangaroo		
potato		
tomato		
risotto		
flamingo		
mango		
armadillo		
volcano		
echo		
cuckoo		
radio		
piano		
cello		
banjo		
igloo		
tattoo		

party	parties
city	cities
puppy	puppies
curry	curries
hobby	hobbies
worry	worries
story	stories
fairy	fairies

Spelling activity sheet

SET 7

SHEET B

NAME: _____

Lots of words end with a consonant followed by a **y**.

When you make a plural, change the **y** to **i** and add **es**.

Write the plural for each of the following words. Put your plural word into an interesting sentence. The first one has been done for you.

1. _worry_ ⟶ _worries_
   Lucky people don't have many worries.

2. hobby ⟶ _____

   _____

3. curry ⟶ _____

   _____

4. puppy ⟶ _____

   _____

5. city ⟶ _____

   _____

6. story ⟶ _____

   _____

7. fairy ⟶ _____

   _____

8. party ⟶ _____

   _____

Make a list of at least 20 words ending with ch, sh, s or x.
Using a dictionary to help you, write the plural of each of your words.

25

Learn, write, check

NAME: _____

Look and say	Write then cover	Write then check
party		
parties		
city		
cities		
puppy		
puppies		
curry		
curries		
hobby		
hobbies		
worry		
worries		
story		
stories		
fairy		
fairies		

life	lives
thief	thieves
scarf	scarves
knife	knives
loaf	loaves
leaf	leaves
sheaf	sheaves
self	selves

© Spelling for Literacy for ages 9-10 • Andrew Brodie 2015 • www.bloomsbury.com

NAME: _____

Words ending in **f** or **fe** use **ves** in their plural.

However, when a word ends in **ff**, you just add an **s**.

Put these words into pairs of singular and plural.
The first one has been done for you.

life	thieves	lives	sheaves
self	knives	leaves	loaf
scarf	loaves	scarves	selves
knife	thief	sheaf	leaf

SINGULAR (ONE)   **PLURAL (MORE THAN ONE)**

life   →   lives

→

→

→

→

→

→

→

Here are the plural words again but this time the vowels are missing from them.
Put the vowels in the correct places.

l _ v _ s   s _ l v _ s   k n _ v _ s

s h _ _ v _ s   s c _ r v _ s   l _ _ v _ s

l _ _ v _ s   t h _ _ v _ s

Learn, write, check

NAME: _____

Look and say	Write then cover	Write then check
life		
lives		
thief		
thieves		
scarf		
scarves		
knife		
knives		
loaf		
loaves		
leaf		
leaves		
sheaf		
sheaves		
self		
selves		

mouse	mice
goose	geese
child	children
man	men
woman	women
fungus	fungi
tooth	teeth
fish	sheep

Spelling activity sheet

NAME: _____

 Some words make their plurals in unusual ways.

 Words such as **fish** and **sheep** are the same in both the singular and plural.

Use the words in the box to complete the puzzles.

mouse	fish	fungi	fungus
mice	men	sheep	children
goose	child	woman	geese
tooth	women	man	teeth

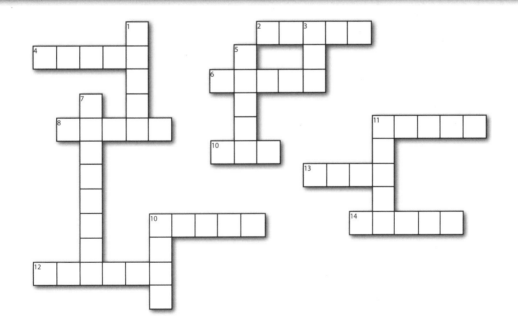

CLUES DOWN:
1 Large web-footed birds.
3 An adult male human being.
5 The male is called a gander.
7 You will find these in a school.
10 Water creatures.
11 These are found in your mouth.

CLUES ACROSS:
2 An adult female human being.
4 Small furry creature.
6 Several adult female human beings.
8 Flock of white woolly animals.
9 Several adult male human beings.
10 Several mushrooms or toadstools.
11 The dentist removed a decayed

_____.
12 A single mushroom or toadstool.
13 Several small furry creatures.
14 A young human being.

Some words are always in their plural form, e.g. 'scissors'. Make a list of words that are always plural and a list of words that remain the same when made plural, such as the word 'fish'.

© Spelling for Literacy for ages 9-10 • Andrew Brodie 2015 • www.bloomsbury.com

Learn, write, check

NAME: _____

Look and say	Write then cover	Write then check
mouse		
mice		
goose		
geese		
child		
children		
man		
men		
woman		
women		
fungus		
fungi		
tooth		
teeth		
fish		
sheep		

32

use	useful
dread	dreadful
care	careful
cheer	cheerful
skill	skilful
colour	colourful
beauty	beautiful
plenty	plentiful

© Spelling for Literacy for ages 9-10 • Andrew Brodie 2015 • www.bloomsbury.com

Spelling activity sheet

NAME: _____

The suffix **ful** simply means **full**.

When adding **ful** to a word ending with a consonant and a **y**, remember to change the **y** to an **i**.

Put the words into pairs. The first one has been done for you.

cheerful	useful	dreadful	colourful
beauty	beautiful	skill	careful
use	dread	plentiful	cheer
skilful	plenty	care	colour

use → useful

_____ → _____

_____ → _____

_____ → _____

_____ → _____

_____ → _____

_____ → _____

_____ → _____

Did you notice that the word 'skill' drops an l before adding 'ful'?

Now arrange your 16 words into alphabetical order.

1 _____   5 _____   9 _____   13 _____

2 _____   6 _____   10 _____   14 _____

3 _____   7 _____   11 _____   15 _____

4 _____   8 _____   12 _____   16 _____

Learn, write, check

NAME: _____

Look and say	Write then cover	Write then check
use		
useful		
dread		
dreadful		
care		
careful		
cheer		
cheerful		
skill		
skilful		
colour		
colourful		
beauty		
beautiful		
plenty		
plentiful		

35

automatic	autopilot
automobile	autobiography
autograph	telepathy
telephone	television
telegraph	telescope
biscuit	bilingual
bicentenary	biceps
binocular	bifocal

Spelling activity sheet

NAME: _____

auto is a prefix meaning **self**.

Something that is automatic works by itself.

Sort the words into lists of 'auto', 'bi' and 'tele' words.

bilingual	biscuit	biceps	television
autobiography	autopilot	telepathy	autograph
telephone	binocular	bicentenary	bifocal
automatic	telegraph	automobile	telescope

auto	bi	tele

Now add one more word to each list. You may need a dictionary to help you.

_____   _____   _____

Use a dictionary to help you to write a definition for each of the 'bi' words. What does the prefix 'bi' mean?

Look particularly carefully for the word 'biscuit'. Can you find out what the prefix 'bi' means in this word?

NAME: _____

Look and say	Write then cover	Write then check
automatic		
autopilot		
automobile		
autobiography		
autograph		
telepathy		
telephone		
television		
telegraph		
telescope		
biscuit		
bilingual		
bicentenary		
biceps		
binocular		
bifocal		

circle	circumference
circular	circus
circuit	circumnavigate
circumscribe	circumstance
transport	transmit
transparent	transparency
transatlantic	translate
transform	translation

Spelling activity sheet

NAME: _____

The prefix **circum** (often shortened to **circ**) means **round**.

The prefix **trans** means **through** or **across**.

Choose four words from each box.
Put each of your eight words into an interesting sentence.

circle	transparent
circus	translate
circuit	transparency
circumstance	translation
circumscribe	transport
circular	transatlantic
circumference	transmit
circumnavigate	transform

1 _____

_____

2 _____

_____

3 _____

_____

4 _____

_____

5 _____

_____

6 _____

_____

7 _____

_____

8 _____

_____

Learn, write, check

NAME: _____

Look and say	Write then cover	Write then check
circle		
circumference		
circular		
circus		
circuit		
circumnavigate		
circumscribe		
circumstance		
transport		
transmit		
transparent		
transparency		
transatlantic		
translate		
transform		
translation		

electric	electricity
electrician	electrical
mechanic	mechanical
mechanism	mechanise
meteor	meteorite
meteorology	meteoric
prison	prisoner
imprisoned	imprisonment

Spelling activity sheet

NAME: _____

Many words have a main part, called the root.

By adding prefixes or suffixes to the root you can change the meaning of the word.

Use the following words to complete the word plants.
Write the root word in the flowerpot, at the root of the plant.

mechanic	meteor	mechanical	electricity
electric	prisoner	prison	imprisonment
mechanise	meteorite	meteoric	mechanism
imprisoned	electrical	electrician	meteorology

meteorology

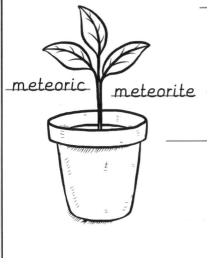

meteoric   meteorite

meteor

**Did you know that you can spell the word mechanise with either an s (mechanise)
or a z (mechanize)? They are both correct.**

Make more word plants from the following roots:

take   public   hand   legal

Learn, write, check

NAME: _____

Look and say	Write then cover	Write then check
electric		
electricity		
electrician		
electrical		
mechanic		
mechanical		
mechanism		
mechanise		
meteor		
meteorite		
meteorology		
meteoric		
prison		
prisoner		
imprisoned		
imprisonment		

cinema	decide
cereal	centre
cylinder	mercy
celebration	December
circulation	cyclone
circumstances	accident
circuit	circle
certificate	circus

NAME: _____

 The letter **c** can sound hard like **k** or soft like **s**.

 **c** usually makes a soft sound when it is followed by **i** or **e**.

Solve the clues to complete this puzzle as it steps down the page.

mercy	cinema	certificate	cereal	cyclone
cylinder	decide	circle	circulation	centre
celebration	circus	circuit	December	

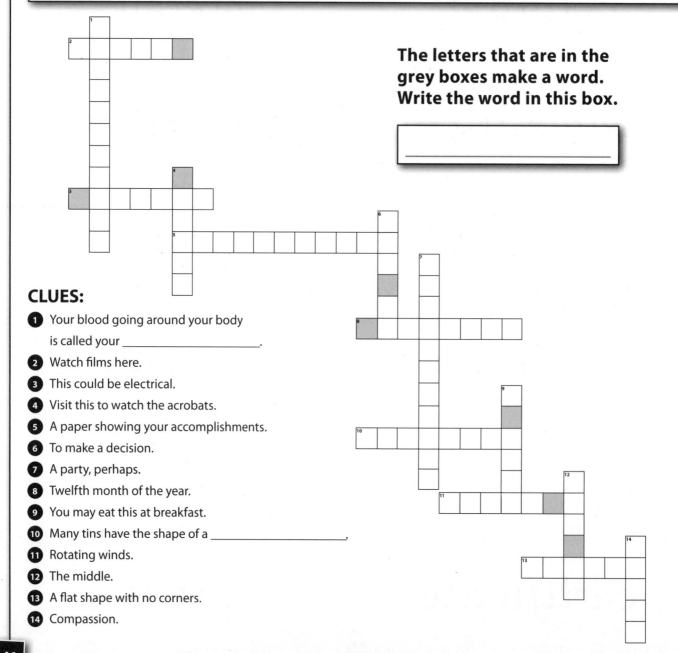

The letters that are in the grey boxes make a word. Write the word in this box.

_____

CLUES:

1. Your blood going around your body is called your _____.
2. Watch films here.
3. This could be electrical.
4. Visit this to watch the acrobats.
5. A paper showing your accomplishments.
6. To make a decision.
7. A party, perhaps.
8. Twelfth month of the year.
9. You may eat this at breakfast.
10. Many tins have the shape of a _____.
11. Rotating winds.
12. The middle.
13. A flat shape with no corners.
14. Compassion.

Learn, write, check

NAME: _____

Look and say	Write then cover	Write then check
cinema		
decide		
cereal		
centre		
cylinder		
mercy		
celebration		
December		
circulation		
cyclone		
circumstances		
accident		
circuit		
circle		
certificate		
circus		

scone	score
scale	cough
collar	container
compass	encourage
cabbage	escape
custard	cucumber
cupboard	cobweb
concerned	concentrate

Spelling activity sheet

NAME: _____

A **c** followed by **a**, **u** or **o** usually makes a hard sound.

Some words can have both the hard **c** and the soft **c** in them.

Below are some words with letter c plus some other words and letters. Take only the <u>words</u> that include a 'c' and put them in the correct boxes.

circumstance	custard	cobweb	mercy	circulation
cinema	ci	scone	decide	score
celebration	cereal	ce	scale	cough
cylinder	and	centre	cy	container
usually	fancy	collar	compass	December
concentrate	escape	soften	concerned	cupboard
the	cyclone	circle	cabbage	certificate
accident	encourage	circus	c	cucumber

SOFT C	HARD C	HARD AND SOFT C

The words and the letter groups that remain should help you remember a spelling rule. Write it here.

_____

Learn, write, check

NAME:

Look and say	Write then cover	Write then check
scone		
score		
scale		
cough		
collar		
container		
compass		
encourage		
cabbage		
escape		
custard		
cucumber		
cupboard		
cobweb		
concerned		
concentrate		

flight	freight
eight	height
sprightly	night
slight	straight
thief	niece
piece	field
lie	fiery
fierce	fiesta

Spelling activity sheet

NAME: _____

 The letter strings **ight**, **ie** and **ei** are found in many words.

 They make different sounds in different words.

Read these words aloud and listen to the sounds made by the 'ie', the 'ei' and the 'ight'.

flight	sprightly	thief	lie
eight	knight	niece	fiery
freight	slight	piece	fierce
height	straight	field	fiesta

Now use the words to help you solve the clues. A rhyming word is also given to help you.

	CLUE	RHYMING WORD	ANSWER
1	How tall I am.	bite	_____
2	Someone who steals.	beef	_____
3	Very hot.	priory	_____
4	An enclosed area of land.	peeled	_____
5	Not curved.	mate	_____
6	Not the truth.	buy	_____
7	He fights with dragons.	write	_____
8	More than seven.	bait	_____

Did you notice that the rhyming words have different letter strings in them?
Find rhyming words with a different spelling pattern for each of the following words.

flight → _____   freight → _____

neice → _____   piece → _____

weight → _____   slight → _____

Working with a friend, make a list of all the 'ight' words you can find. You should have at least 20. Now split them into groups according to the sound the 'ight' makes.

Learn, write, check

SET 16
SHEET C

NAME: _____

Look and say	Write then cover	Write then check
flight		
freight		
eight		
height		
sprightly		
night		
slight		
straight		
thief		
niece		
piece		
field		
lie		
fiery		
fierce		
fiesta		

53

earth	heart
fearsome	hearth
beard	smear
search	yearn
four	neighbour
flour	colour
hour	mourn
tour	honourable

54

Spelling activity sheet

NAME: _____

The letters **ear** sound quite different in the words **heart** and **bear**.

The letters **our** sound different in **flour** and **four**.

All the following words should have either 'ear' or 'our' in them. Put in the correct set of letters to make each word complete.

f _ _ _   h _ _ _ t h   t _ _ _

s m _ _ _   n e i g h b _ _ _   h _ _ _

b _ _ _ d   f _ _ _ s o m e   s _ _ _ c h

_ _ _ t h   h _ _ _   h _ _ _ t

f l _ _ _   t _ _ _   m _ _ _ n

c o l _ _ _   f _ _ _

h o n _ _ _ a b l e   y _ _ _ n

Choose a word from above for each of the following clues.

1. One plus three.   → _____

2. To grieve.   → _____

3. Facial hair.   → _____

4. Red and yellow are examples of this.   → _____

5. Pumps blood around the body.   → _____

6. In front of the fire.   → _____

7. Sixty minutes.   → _____

8. Lives next door.   → _____

9. To hunt.   → _____

10. Use this in cooking.   → _____

NAME: _____

Look and say	Write then cover	Write then check
earth		
heart		
fearsome		
hearth		
beard		
smear		
search		
yearn		
four		
neighbour		
flour		
colour		
hour		
mourn		
tour		
honourable		

scene	seen
cereal	serial
where	wear
tear	tier
knight	night
grate	great
key	quay
pane	pain

NAME: _____

 Some words sound exactly the same but have different spellings and different meanings.

 These words are known as homophones.

Use the words to label the pictures.

| tier | key | quay | tear |

 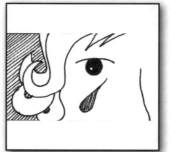  

Now draw your own illustrations in these boxes.

| scene | seen | knight | night |

| where | wear | great | grate |

Can you think of six more pairs of homophones and illustrate them?

Learn, write, check

NAME:

Look and say	Write then cover	Write then check
scene		
seen		
cereal		
serial		
where		
wear		
tear		
tier		
knight		
night		
grate		
great		
key		
quay		
pane		
pain		

electrician	optician
magician	politician
physician	musician
ration	station
invitation	multiplication
creation	elation
foundation	translation
communication	education

Spelling activity sheet

NAME: _____

ation and **cian** are common word endings.

Although they sound very similar they are spelled quite differently.

Choose words to complete each sentence correctly.

electrician	invitation	magician	communication
ration	education	musician	optician
station	translation	creation	physician
politician	foundations	elation	multiplication

1 I visited the _____ to have my eyes tested.

2 The train left the _____ on time.

3 The _____ pulled a rabbit out of a hat.

4 I have had an _____ to a party.

5 The builder laid the _____ of the house and the _____ did the wiring.

6 In maths today we did some _____.

7 A _____ is a doctor.

8 I read a _____ of a book that had originally been written in a foreign language.

Did you notice that the 'cian' words told us about jobs people do? Other word endings that help us understand jobs are 'er'(teacher), 'or' (doctor) and 'ist' (artist). Make four lists of jobs under the headings.

cian	or	er	ist
_____	_____	_____	_____
_____	_____	_____	_____
_____	_____	_____	_____
_____	_____	_____	_____

Learn, write, check

NAME: _____

Look and say	Write then cover	Write then check
electrician		
optician		
magician		
politician		
physician		
musician		
ration		
station		
invitation		
multiplication		
creation		
elation		
foundation		
translation		
communication		
education		

62

reflection	section
correction	direction
attraction	distraction
fiction	faction
sanction	reduction
diction	fraction
collection	construction
infection	traction

Spelling activity sheet

NAME: _____

Many words have the suffix **tion** following a consonant.

Often the **tion** follows the letter **c**.

Sort the words into two boxes. One should contain all the 'tion' words. The other should contain those words with other endings that sound like 'tion' but are spelled differently.

reflection	session	passion	extension
cushion	traction	reduction	distraction
construction	fashion	permission	fraction
sanction	correction	collection	magician
confession	mansion	infection	attraction
section	diction	progression	mission
musician	direction	faction	fiction

TION

_____ _____
_____ _____
_____ _____
_____ _____
_____ _____
_____ _____
_____ _____

OTHERS

_____ _____
_____ _____
_____ _____
_____ _____
_____ _____
_____ _____

Choose words from the 'tion' box to solve the clues.

1. See this in a mirror. ⟶ _____
2. The way a person speaks. ⟶ _____
3. A punishment or penalty. ⟶ _____
4. Part of a whole. ⟶ _____

Use a dictionary to help you to write a definition for each of the remaining words from the 'tion' box.

Learn, write, check

NAME:  _____

Look and say	Write then cover	Write then check
reflection		
section		
correction		
direction		
attraction		
distraction		
fiction		
faction		
sanction		
reduction		
diction		
fraction		
collection		
construction		
infection		
traction		

aggression	session
confession	impression
depression	percussion
mission	passion
possession	dispossession
progression	profession
discussion	oppression
permission	procession

Spelling activity sheet

NAME: _____

Another fairly common ending is **ssion**.

Many of the root words already end with **ss**.

Use the words in the box to give each of the root words below a partner.
The first one has been done for you.

depression	discussion	permission	percussion	procession
possession	confession	dispossession	profession	impression

1. confess ⟶ confession
2. depress ⟶ _____
3. possess ⟶ _____
4. dispossess ⟶ _____
5. profess ⟶ _____
6. discuss ⟶ _____
7. process ⟶ _____
8. impress ⟶ _____
9. percuss ⟶ _____
10. permit ⟶ _____

Illustrate each of the words in the boxes below to show you understand their meanings.

aggression	**percussion**	**discussion**	**procession**

Work with a friend to make an alphabetical list of 'ssion' words.
You may need to use a dictionary.

A ⟶ aggression

Which letters could you not find any 'ssion' words for?

Learn, write, check

NAME: _____

Look and say	Write then cover	Write then check
aggression		
session		
confession		
impression		
depression		
percussion		
mission		
passion		
possession		
dispossession		
progression		
profession		
discussion		
oppression		
permission		
procession		

mansion	explosion
occasion	conclusion
division	extension
confusion	decision
collision	television
vision	invasion
expansion	revision
exclusion	inclusion

Spelling activity sheet

NAME: _____

 The suffix **sion** is found on many words.

 It can follow both consonants and vowels.

Illustrate the following words.

aggression	percussion	discussion	procession

Using the words in the box, match the root word to its partner.
The first one has been done for you.

confusion	expansion	collision	division
decision	exclusion	extension	explosion
invasion	revision	conclusion	inclusion

1. explode _____explosion_____
2. conclude _____
3. divide _____
4. extend _____
5. confuse _____
6. exclude _____

7. decide _____
8. collide _____
9. invade _____
10. expand _____
11. revise _____
12. include _____

Make a list of all the 'sion' words you can find. Beside each word, write its root word.

70

Learn, write, check

NAME: _____

Look and say	Write then cover	Write then check
mansion		
explosion		
occasion		
conclusion		
division		
extension		
confusion		
decision		
collision		
television		
vision		
invasion		
expansion		
revision		
exclusion		
inclusion		

dilution	pollution
contribution	distribution
expedition	addition
repetition	position
condition	competition
lotion	potion
promotion	devotion
completion	deletion

Spelling activity sheet

NAME: _____

This page has more **tion** suffixes.

Each **tion** on this page follows one of the vowels **e**, **i**, **o** or **u**.

Sort the words according to which vowel comes before the 'tion' and place them under the correct headings. Try to find one new word to add to each list.

lotion	dilution	addition	devotion
distribution	competition	contribution	pollution
condition	completion	potion	expedition
promotion	deletion	position	repetition

etion	**ition**	**otion**	**ution**

Choose one word from each list to put into an interesting sentence.

1 _____

_____

2 _____

_____

3 _____

_____

4 _____

_____

Learn, write, check

NAME:

Look and say	Write then cover	Write then check
dilution		
pollution		
contribution		
distribution		
expedition		
addition		
repetition		
position		
condition		
competition		
lotion		
potion		
promotion		
devotion		
completion		
deletion		

jewellery	explanatory
voluntary	dictionary
factory	literacy
library	definitely
miserable	literature
interested	desperate
generous	marvellous
Wednesday	familiar

75

Spelling activity sheet

NAME: _____

The words on this page have vowels that are not always heard when the word is said.

This makes these words quite tricky to spell.

Read the words aloud. Circle any vowels that you cannot hear clearly when the word is said.

jewellery	factory	miserable	generous
explanatory	literacy	literature	marvellous
voluntary	library	interested	Wednesday
dictionary	definitely	desperate	familiar

Now choose a word from the box to fill each of the blanks in the sentences below.

1 I went to the _____ to borrow a book.

2 The days of the week are Monday, Tuesday, _____, Thursday, Friday, Saturday and Sunday.

3 Work that is unpaid is called _____.

4 Use a _____ to check your spellings.

5 I am _____ in wildlife.

6 You can buy _____ in a jeweller's shop.

Make a list of 10 words ending in 'ary' or 'ery'.
Read your words aloud and circle any vowels that cannot be clearly heard.

_____ _____ _____

_____ _____ _____

_____ _____

Learn, write, check

NAME: _____

Look and say	Write then cover	Write then check
jewellery		
explanatory		
voluntary		
dictionary		
factory		
literacy		
library		
definitely		
miserable		
literature		
interested		
desperate		
generous		
marvellous		
Wednesday		
familiar		

© Spelling for Literacy for ages 9-10 • Andrew Brodie 2015 • www.bloomsbury.com

generally	interest
poisonous	secretary
separate	business
boundary	difference
original	company
different	centre
frightening	general
offering	family

Spelling activity sheet

NAME: _____

Here are some more words that cannot be spelled just by listening to them.

This is because when they are spoken not all of the vowels can be clearly heard.

Look at the words in the box and read them aloud.
Circle any vowels that cannot be heard clearly.

generally	separate	original	frightening
interest	business	company	general
poisonous	boundary	different	offering
secretary	difference	centre	family

Now arrange the words in alphabetical order.

1 _____   2 _____
3 _____   4 _____
5 _____   6 _____
7 _____   8 _____
9 _____   10 _____
11 _____   12 _____
13 _____   14 _____
15 _____   16 _____

Select two of the words then, with the help of a dictionary, write a definition of your chosen words.

_____ _____

_____ _____

_____ _____

_____ _____

Learn, write, check

NAME: _____

Look and say	Write then cover	Write then check
generally		
interest		
poisonous		
secretary		
separate		
business		
boundary		
difference		
original		
company		
different		
centre		
frightening		
general		
offering		
family		

proper	improper
mature	immature
patient	impatient
polite	impolite
attentive	inattentive
convenient	inconvenient
accurate	inaccurate
active	inactive

Spelling activity sheet

NAME: _____

The prefixes **im** and **in** mean not.

You will probably find **im** before words beginning with **m** or **p**.

Put the words from the box into pairs. The first pair has been done for you.

improper	inattentive	impolite	inaccurate
convenient	accurate	proper	active
polite	impractical	mature	impatient
patient	inactive	practical	inconvenient
credible	incredible	attentive	immature

proper → improper   _____ → _____

_____ → _____   _____ → _____

_____ → _____   _____ → _____

_____ → _____   _____ → _____

_____ → _____   _____ → _____

Now choose the words from the box that mean the same or nearly the same as the words or phrases below.

1. lively   ⟶ _____
2. well mannered   ⟶ _____
3. not lively   ⟶ _____
4. not well mannered   ⟶ _____
5. paying attention   ⟶ _____
6. not paying attention   ⟶ _____
7. fully developed   ⟶ _____
8. not yet fully developed   ⟶ _____

NAME: _____

Look and say	Write then cover	Write then check
proper		
improper		
mature		
immature		
patient		
impatient		
polite		
impolite		
attentive		
inattentive		
convenient		
inconvenient		
accurate		
inaccurate		
active		
inactive		

logical	illogical
legal	illegal
literate	illiterate
legible	illegible
relevant	irrelevant
regular	irregular
removable	irremovable
replaceable	irreplaceable

Spelling activity sheet

NAME: _____

The prefix **il** means **not** and is found before words starting with an **l**.

The prefix **ir** also means **not** and is found before words starting with an **r**.

Read these words aloud and listen to the sounds made by the 'ie' and the 'ight'.

relevant	irreplaceable	illiterate	illegal
removable	literate	irregular	irremovable
legal	regular	illegible	illogical
logical	replaceable	legible	irrelevant

Fill in the spaces below using the words from the box above. Use the clues to help you.

WORD   **CLUE**

1 _____ Methodical

2 _____ Against the law

3 _____ Able to read

4 _____ It is impossible to get another one

5 _____ Impossible to read this writing

6 _____ Done at odd intervals

7 _____ Unable to read

8 _____ You cannot remove this

Which words from the box did you not use?

_____ _____ _____ _____

_____ _____ _____ _____

Try to think of a clue for each of these words. Make a word puzzle like the one on this page. Give the puzzle to a friend to complete.

Learn, write, check

NAME: _____

Look and say	Write then cover	Write then check
logical		
illogical		
legal		
illegal		
literate		
illiterate		
legible		
illegible		
relevant		
irrelevant		
regular		
irregular		
removable		
irremovable		
replaceable		
irreplaceable		

vice	vicious
grace	gracious
space	spacious
precious	conscious
delicious	malice
malicious	suspicious
ambitious	caution
cautious	fictitious

Spelling activity sheet

NAME: _____

Some of these words end with **cious** and some end with **tious**.

If the root word ends in **ce**, the ending is usually **cious**.

Put the words from the box into pairs. The first pair has been done for you.

vice	space	delicious	ambitious
vicious	spacious	malice	caution
grace	precious	malicious	cautious
gracious	conscious	suspicious	fictitious

Write the correct 'cious' or 'tious' word for each root word shown.

malice ⟶ malicious   vice ⟶ _____

space ⟶ _____   ambition ⟶ _____

caution ⟶ _____   suspicion ⟶ _____

grace ⟶ _____   fiction ⟶ _____

Write the missing words.

There is plenty of room in the hall as it is very

_____.

The _____ dog barked loudly. It made
me nervous so I was very _____.

I like reading _____ books.

Diamonds are very _____ jewels.

The dinner was _____.

I am quite _____ because when I grow
up I want a really good job.

Learn, write, check

NAME:

Look and say	Write then cover	Write then check
vice		
vicious		
grace		
gracious		
space		
spacious		
precious		
conscious		
delicious		
malice		
malicious		
suspicious		
ambitious		
caution		
cautious		
fictitious		

official	special
artificial	partial
confidential	essential
initial	financial
commercial	provincial
anxiety	anxious
infect	infectious
infection	nutritious

Spelling activity sheet

NAME: _____

 The ending **cial** usually comes after a vowel but sometimes after a consonant.

 The ending **tial** usually comes after a consonant.

official	confidential	commercial	infect
special	essential	provincial	infectious
artificial	initial	anxiety	infection
partial	financial	anxious	nutritious

Sort the words into sets.

cial	tial	ious	ion
_____	_____	_____	_____
_____	_____	_____	
_____	_____	_____	
_____	_____		
_____			
_____			

Which two words did not fit into any of the sets?

_____   _____

Write three sentences using as many of the words as possible.

_____

_____

_____

_____

_____

Learn, write, check

NAME: _____

Look and say	Write then cover	Write then check
official		
special		
artificial		
partial		
confidential		
essential		
initial		
financial		
commercial		
provincial		
anxiety		
anxious		
infect		
infectious		
infection		
nutritious		

observe	observant
observance	observation
expectant	expectation
hesitate	hesitant
hesitancy	hesitation
tolerate	tolerant
tolerance	toleration
substance	substantial

Spelling activity sheet

NAME: _____

 Some root words have lots of derivatives.

 Derivatives are words created from other words.

observe	expectant	substantial	hesitancy
expectation	observant	hesitation	toleration
hesitate	tolerate	observance	substance
tolerance	hesitant	tolerant	observation

Write as many derivatives as you can for each root word.
Some of the derivatives are not shown in the box.

observe
_____
_____
_____
_____
_____
_____

expect
_____
_____
_____
_____
_____
_____

hesitate
_____
_____
_____
_____
_____

tolerate
_____ _____
_____ _____
_____ _____
_____ _____
_____

substance
_____
_____
_____
_____
_____

94

Learn, write, check

NAME:

Look and say	Write then cover	Write then check
observe		
observant		
observance		
observation		
expectant		
expectation		
hesitate		
hesitant		
hesitancy		
hesitation		
tolerate		
tolerant		
tolerance		
toleration		
substance		
substantial		

innocent	innocence
innocently	decent
decency	frequent
frequency	confident
confidence	confidential
assistant	assistance
obedient	obedience
independent	independence

NAME: _____

 The endings **ent**, **ence** and **ency** can be used after a soft **c** sound or a soft **g** sound...

 ...and after **qu**.

innocent	decency	confidence	obedient
innocence	frequent	confidential	obedience
innocently	frequency	assistant	independent
decent	confident	assistance	independence

Which two words in the box do not contain 'ent', 'ence' or 'ency'?

_____   _____

Now sort the other words.

ent	ence	ency

Can you think of another word related to each of the following words?

frequent _____   obedient _____

confident _____   independent _____

Learn, write, check

NAME: _____

Look and say	Write then cover	Write then check
innocent		
innocence		
innocently		
decent		
decency		
frequent		
frequency		
confident		
confidence		
confidential		
assistant		
assistance		
obedient		
obedience		
independent		
independence		

refer	referring
referred	referral
prefer	preferring
preferred	transfer
transferring	transferred
transference	transferable
reference	referee
preference	preferable

Spelling activity sheet

NAME: _____

You need to double the **r** if the **fer** is still stressed when an ending is added.

You don't need to double the **r** if the **fer** is not stressed.

In the word 'refer', the 'fer' part is stressed and it is still stressed in the words 'referring', 'referred' or 'referral', where the r is doubled. When the 'fer' is not stressed, like in the words 'reference' or 'referee', the r is not doubled.

Find some words derived from each of the root words.

refer	prefer	transfer
_____	_____	_____
_____	_____	_____
_____	_____	_____
_____	_____	_____
	_____	

Write three sentences using some of the words you have written above.

_____

_____

_____

_____

_____

_____

Learn, write, check

NAME: _____

Look and say	Write then cover	Write then check
refer		
referring		
referred		
referral		
prefer		
preferring		
preferred		
transfer		
transferring		
transferred		
transference		
transferable		
reference		
referee		
preference		
preferable		

accommodate	accommodation
accompany	accompaniment
according	achieve
aggressive	amateur
ancient	apparent
appreciate	appreciation
attached	attachment
available	availability

Spelling activity sheet

NAME: _____

The words on this page…

…are important words to learn!

accommodate	according	ancient	attached
accommodation	achieve	apparent	attachment
accompany	aggressive	appreciate	available
accompaniment	amateur	appreciation	availability

Write the correct word in each gap.

I am not a professional artist, I am an _____.

When we arrived on holiday, the first thing we needed was to find our _____.

The pyramids in Egypt are _____ monuments.

Could I check the _____ of tickets for the concert?

The piano was the perfect _____ for the singer.

The photograph arrived as an _____ to the email.

Write two sentences of your own, including some of the words from the word bank.

_____

_____

_____

_____

© Spelling for Literacy for ages 9-10 • Andrew Brodie 2015 • www.bloomsbury.com

Learn, write, check

NAME: _____

Look and say	Write then cover	Write then check
accommodate		
accommodation		
accompany		
accompaniment		
according		
achieve		
aggressive		
amateur		
ancient		
apparent		
appreciate		
appreciation		
attached		
attachment		
available		
availability		

average	awkward
bargain	bruise
category	cemetery
committee	communicate
communication	community
competition	competitive
conscience	conscious
controversy	controversial

Spelling activity sheet

NAME: _____

Here are more important words to learn.

Some of them are quite tricky.

average	category	communication	conscience
awkward	cemetery	community	conscious
bargain	committee	competition	controversy
bruise	communicate	competitive	controversial

Write the correct word in each gap.

The new camera was quite cheap so it was a real _____.

I was very excited when I won the first prize in the _____.

There are lots of old gravestones in the _____.

'Stop being so _____!' said my mum when I wouldn't eat my dinner.

The children were keen to take part in the race because they are very _____.

Email is a very useful method of _____.

Write two sentences of your own, including some of the words from the word bank.

_____

_____

_____

_____

Learn, write, check

NAME: _____

Look and say	Write then cover	Write then check
average		
awkward		
bargain		
bruise		
category		
cemetery		
committee		
communicate		
communication		
community		
competition		
competitive		
conscience		
conscious		
controversy		
controversial		

convenience	conveniently
correspond	correspondence
critic	critical
criticise	curiosity
curious	definite
definition	desperate
determined	develop
dictionary	disastrous

Spelling activity sheet

NAME: _____

How many of these words do you know?

I know most of them!

convenience	critic	curious	determined
conveniently	critical	definite	develop
correspond	criticise	definition	dictionary
correspondence	curiosity	desperate	disastrous

Write the correct word in each gap.

The bus stopped _____ right next to the park.

It's not nice to _____ other people.

'Can you give me the _____ of this word?' asked the teacher.

'Only if I look it up in the _____,' I replied.

The cat was _____ about the scuffling noise in the undergrowth.

The girl was _____ to win the prize.

Write two sentences of your own, including some of the words from the word bank.

_____

_____

_____

_____

NAME: _____

Look and say	Write then cover	Write then check
convenience		
conveniently		
correspond		
correspondence		
critic		
critical		
criticise		
curiosity		
curious		
definite		
definition		
desperate		
determined		
develop		
dictionary		
disastrous		

embarrass	environment
equip	equipped
equipment	especially
exaggerate	exaggeration
excellence	excellent
existence	explanation
familiar	foreign
forty	frequently

Spelling activity sheet

NAME: _____

It's strange that the number words **four** and **fourteen** have a letter **u**…

…but the word **forty** doesn't.

embarrass	equipment	excellence	familiar
environment	especially	excellent	foreign
equip	exaggerate	existence	forty
equipped	exaggeration	explanation	frequently

Write the correct word in each gap.

The teacher said my work was _____.

It is very important to look after the _____.

The headteacher told the boy off for playing with the science _____.

'Can you give me a good _____ for why you are late?' asked the teacher.

One hundred subtract sixty is _____.

I asked my dad not to _____ me by telling silly jokes.

Write two sentences of your own, including some of the words from the word bank.

_____

_____

_____

_____

112

Learn, write, check

NAME: _____

Look and say	Write then cover	Write then check
embarrass		
environment		
equip		
equipped		
equipment		
especially		
exaggerate		
exaggeration		
excellence		
excellent		
existence		
explanation		
familiar		
foreign		
forty		
frequently		

government	guarantee
harass	hindrance
identity	identification
immediate	immediately
individual	interfere
interrupt	language
leisure	lightning
marvellous	mischief

Spelling activity sheet

NAME: _____

It's strange that the word guarantee has a letter **u**…

…and so does the word **guard**.

government	identity	individual	leisure
guarantee	identification	interfere	lightning
harass	immediate	interrupt	marvellous
hindrance	immediately	language	mischief

Write the correct word in each gap.

'It's very rude to _____!' said the teacher crossly.

The new bike had a two year _____.

'Try not to _____ your little brother,' said my mum.

I had to show some _____ at the bank.

'Come here _____!' called the lady to her dog.

Swimming is one of my favourite _____ activities.

Write two sentences of your own, including some of the words from the word bank.

_____

_____

_____

_____

Learn, write, check

NAME: _____

Look and say	Write then cover	Write then check
government		
guarantee		
harass		
hindrance		
identity		
identification		
immediate		
immediately		
individual		
interfere		
interrupt		
language		
leisure		
lightning		
marvellous		
mischief		

mischievous	muscle
necessary	necessarily
neighbour	nuisance
occupy	occupation
occur	opportunity
parliament	persuade
persuasion	physical
prejudice	privilege

NAME: _____

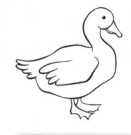

Look carefully at the word **mischievous**.

The letter **i** only appears twice in the word.

mischievous	neighbour	occur	persuasion
muscle	nuisance	opportunity	physical
necessary	occupy	parliament	prejudice
necessarily	occupation	persuade	privilege

Write the correct word in each gap.

The man was showing off the _____ in his right arm.

I would like the _____ to travel to America.

The government meets in the Houses of _____.

We wear shorts and t-shirts for _____ education.

The boy's behaviour was always _____.

It was a great _____ to meet the queen.

Write two sentences of your own, including some of the words from the word bank.

_____

_____

_____

_____

Learn, write, check

NAME:

Look and say	Write then cover	Write then check
mischievous		
muscle		
necessary		
necessarily		
neighbour		
nuisance		
occupy		
occupation		
occur		
opportunity		
parliament		
persuade		
persuasion		
physical		
prejudice		
privilege		

profession	programme
pronounce	pronunciation
queue	recognise
recognition	recommend
relevant	restaurant
rhyme	rhythm
sacrifice	secretary
shoulder	signature

Spelling activity sheet

NAME: _____

The word **rhythm** is very unusual...

...because it doesn't include any vowels.

profession	queue	relevant	sacrifice
programme	recognise	restaurant	secretary
pronounce	recognition	rhyme	shoulder
pronunciation	recommend	rhythm	signature

Write the correct word in each gap.

We had our lunch in a fast food _____.

I saw a great _____ on the television.

The _____ typed the letter very carefully.

The toddler asked for the nursery _____
over and over again.

The pirate had a parrot sitting on his _____.

Drums are often used to keep the _____
in music.

Write two sentences of your own, including some of the words from the word bank.

_____

_____

_____

_____

NAME: _____

Look and say	Write then cover	Write then check
profession		
programme		
pronounce		
pronunciation		
queue		
recognise		
recognition		
recommend		
relevant		
restaurant		
rhyme		
rhythm		
sacrifice		
secretary		
shoulder		
signature		

sincere	sincerely
soldier	stomach
sufficient	suggest
symbol	system
systematic	temperature
thorough	twelfth
variety	vegetable
vehicle	yacht

Spelling activity sheet

NAME: _____

The letter **y** makes different sounds in some of these words.

Listen to the sound it makes in **sincerely**, **system** and **yacht**.

sincere	sufficient	systematic	variety
sincerely	suggest	temperature	vegetable
soldier	symbol	thorough	vehicle
stomach	system	twelfth	yacht

Write the correct word in each gap.

The _____ marched up and down in front of the palace.

I like a wide _____ of fruit and vegetables.

It felt very chilly after the sudden drop in the _____.

'I think you've had quite _____!' said my mum when I asked for more ice-cream.

The big car was a very comfortable _____.

My birthday is on the _____ of February.

Write two sentences of your own, including some of the words from the word bank.

_____

_____

_____

_____

Learn, write, check

NAME:

Look and say	Write then cover	Write then check
sincere		
sincerely		
soldier		
stomach		
sufficient		
suggest		
symbol		
system		
systematic		
temperature		
thorough		
twelfth		
variety		
vegetable		
vehicle		
yacht		

Answers

Set 1 Sheet B, p7

bring > brought
fight > fought
buy > bought

Set 2 Sheet B, p10

ow: plough bough
uff: tough roughly toughen enough rough roughen
o: though although dough
or: thought thoughtful
off: cough
oo: through
u: thorough thoroughly borough

Missing words: thought thoroughly cough rough through plough dough

Set 3 Sheet B, p13

horrible horribly impossible impossibly incredible incredibly possible possibly probable probably sensible sensibly terrible terribly visible visibly

impossibility probability visibility sensibility

Set 4 Sheet B, p16

apply applicable applicably application
consider considerable considerably consideration
tolerate tolerable tolerably toleration

remove: removing removed removable
restore: restoring restored restoration restorable

Set 5 Sheet B, p19

FOOD: paella pizza banana
PLACES: Asia Africa America Alabama
CREATURES: koala puma tarantula gorilla
OTHER WORDS: samba camera umbrella fiesta sauna siesta bacteria gala sofa

Set 6 Sheet B, p22

1 kangaroo	9 tomato
2 echo	10 mango
3 cello	11 cuckoo
4 igloo	12 flamingo
5 risotto	13 volcano
6 armadillo	14 radio
7 potato	15 piano
8 tattoo	16 banjo

Set 7 Sheet B, p25

hobbies
curries
puppies
cities
stories
fairies
parties

Pupils write their own sentences using the plural words.
Pupils find at least 20 words and their plurals.

Set 8 Sheet B, p28

life > lives
thief > thieves
self > selves
scarf > scarves
knife > knives
loaf > loaves
sheaf > sheaves
leaf > leaves

lives selves knives
shelves scarves leaves
loaves thieves

Set 9 Sheet B, p31

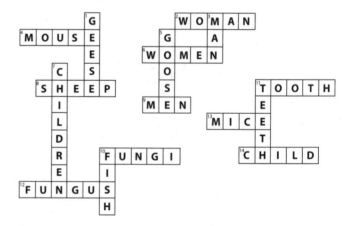

Set 10 Sheet B, p34

skill > skilful
cheer > cheerful
dread > dreadful
care > careful
colour > colourful
beauty > beautiful
plenty > plentiful

1 beauty	5 cheer	9 dread	13 skill
2 beautiful	6 cheerful	10 dreadful	14 skilful
3 care	7 colour	11 plenty	15 use
4 careful	8 colourful	12 plentiful	16 useful

Answers

Set 11 Sheet B, p37

auto: autobiography autobahn autograph automatic automobile
bi: bilingual biscuit biceps binocular bicentenary bifocal
tele: television telepathy telephone telegraph telescope

auto: autopilot
bi: biography
tele: teleconference

The prefix bi relates to two.
The prefix bi in biscuit means twice (because a biscuit used to be 'twice cooked').

Set 12 Sheet B, p40

Pupils create their own sentences using the words.

Set 13 Sheet B, p43

machine: mechanic mechanical mechanise (or mechanize) mechanism
electric: electricity electrical electrician
prison: prisoner imprisoned imprisonment

take: taken took taking intake
public: publicity publish publication
hand: handed handful handsome handy handily
legal: illegal legality legally

Set 14 Sheet B, p46

1 circulation	6 decide	11 cyclone
2 cinema	7 celebration	12 centre
3 circuit	8 December	13 circle
4 circus	9 cereal	14 mercy
5 certificate	10 cylinder	

Missing word: accident

Set 15 Sheet B, p49

SOFT C

decide	celebration	cinema
December	mercy	fancy
centre	cereal	cylinder

HARD C

custard	cabbage	scone
score	encourage	compass
cobweb	scale	escape
cupboard	cough	cucumber
container	collar	

HARD AND SOFT C

circumstance	circle	certificate
concerned	accident	circus
cyclone	circulation	concentrate

The spelling rule will say: ci ce and cy usually soften the c

Set 16 Sheet B, p52

1 height
2 thief
3 fiery
4 field
5 straight
6 lie
7 knight
8 eight

flight > height
freight > wait
neice > fleece
piece > peace
weight > gate
slight > site

Set 17 Sheet B, p55

fear/four	hearth	tear/tour
smear	neighbor	hear
beard	fearsome	search
earth	hear/hour	heart
flour	tour/tear	mourn
colour	four/fear	honourable yearn

1 four	6 hearth
2 mourn	7 hour
3 beard	8 neighbour
4 colour	9 search
5 heart	10 flour

Set 18 Sheet B, p58

Pupils to label pictures and to draw appropriate pictures.

Set 19 Sheet B, p61

1 optician
2 station
3 magician
4 invitation
5 foundation > electrician
6 multiplication
7 physician
8 translation

cian: electrician optician magician beautician mathematician paediatrician
or: doctor conductor illustrator actor decorator
er: painter driver manager teacher
ist: artist scientist chemist dentist

127

Answers

Set 20 Sheet B, p64

TION: reflection construction sanction section traction correction diction direction reduction collection infection faction distraction fraction
attraction fiction

OTHERS: cushion confession musician session fashion mansion passion permission progression extension magician mission

Definitions to be written for:
1 reflection 2 diction 3 sanction 4 fraction

Set 21 Sheet B, p67

2 depression
3 possession
4 dispossession
5 profession
6 discussion
7 procession
8 impression
9 percussion
10 permission

Pupils will probably not find any 'ssion' words beginning with b, g, h, j, k, l, q, u, v, w, x, y or z but should be able to find many others.

Set 22 Sheet B, p70

2 conclusion
3 division
4 extension
5 confusion
6 exclusion
7 decision
8 collision
9 invasion
10 expansion
11 revision
12 inclusion

Set 23 Sheet B, p73

etion: completion deletion
ition: addition competition condition expedition position repetition
otion: lotion devotion potion promotion
ution: dilution distribution contribution pollution

Set 24 Sheet B, p76

1 library
2 Wednesday
3 voluntary
4 dictionary
5 interested
6 jewellery

ary: anniversary boundary burglary canary confectionary customary estuary friary granary imaginary momentary ordinary primary stationary
ery: archery bakery battery celery cemetery confectionery delivery every gallery machinery recovery scenery slippery stationery

Set 25 Sheet B, p79

1 boundary
2 business
3 centre
4 company
5 difference
6 different
7 family
8 frightening
9 general
10 generally
11 interest
12 offering
13 original
14 poisonous
15 secretary
16 separate

Set 26 Sheet B, p82

attentive > inattentive
accurate > inaccurate
polite > impolite
convenient > inconvenient
active > inactive
practical > impractical
mature > immature
patient > impatient
credible > incredible

1 active
2 polite
3 inactive
4 impolite
5 attentive
6 inattentive
7 mature
8 immature

Set 27 Sheet B, p85

1 logical
2 illegal
3 literate
4 irreplaceable
5 illegible
6 irregular
7 illiterate
8 irremovable

relevant removable legal regular illogical replaceable legible irrelevant

Answers

Set 28 Sheet B, p88

vicious
spacious
ambitious
cautious
suspicious
gracious
fictitious

Missing words: spacious vicious cautious fiction precious delicious ambitious

Set 29 Sheet B, p91

cial: official commercial special provincial artificial financial
tial: confidential essential initial partial
ious: infectious nutritious anxious
ion: infection

infect   anxiety

Set 30 Sheet B, p94

observe: observant observance observation observing observatory observer observable observably
expect: expectant expectance expectation expectantly expecting expected expectable expectorant
hesitate: hesitant hesitancy hesitation hesitated hesitating hesitance hesitative
tolerate: tolerant tolerance toleration tolerating tolerated intolerant intolerance tolerator tolerantly tolerable tolerably tolerableness tolerability
substance: substantial substantially substantiate

Set 31 Sheet B, p97

assistant assistance

ent: innocent obedient frequent innocently independent decent confident confidential
ence: confidence innocence obedience independence
ency: decency frequency

frequent: frequently
obedient: obediently
confident: confidently
independent: independently

Set 32 Sheet B, p100

refer: referred referring referral referee reference
prefer: preferred preferring preference preferably preferably preferential preferentially
transfer: transferred transferring transferable transference transferral

Set 33 Sheet B, p103

amateur accommodation ancient availability accompaniment attachment

Set 34 Sheet B, p106

bargain competition cemetery awkward competitive communication

Set 35 Sheet B, p109

conveniently criticise definition dictionary curious determined

Set 36 Sheet B, p112

excellent environment equipment explanation forty embarrass

Set 38 Sheet B, p115

interrupt guarantee harass identification immediately leisure

Set 39 Sheet B, p118

muscle opportunity Parliament physical mischievous privilege

Set 39 Sheet B, p121

restaurant programme rhyme shoulder rhythm

Set 40 Sheet B, p124

soldier variety temperature sufficient vehicle twelfth

Summary

You may wish to photocopy this page and cut it into sets, so that you can give your children a list of the words they will be focusing on each week.

Set 1

ought
buy
bought
think
thought
thoughtful
thoughtfully
thoughtfulness
thoughtless
thoughtlessly
thoughtlessness
nought
bring
brought
fight
fought

Set 2

tough
toughen
enough
cough
though
although
dough
through
thorough
thoroughly
borough
plough
bough
rough
roughen
roughly

Set 3

possible
possibly
impossible
impossibly
horrible
horribly
terrible
terribly
visible
visibly
incredible
incredibly
sensible
sensibly
probable
probably

Set 4

adore
adorable
adorably
adoration
apply
applicable
applicably
application
consider
considerable
considerably
consideration
tolerate
tolerable
tolerably
toleration

Set 5

banana
camera
umbrella
koala
tarantula
sofa
area
gala
puma
pizza
samba
sauna
siesta
fiesta
bacteria
paella

Set 6

kangaroo
potato
tomato
risotto
flamingo
mango
armadillo
volcano
echo
cuckoo
radio
piano
cello
banjo
igloo
tattoo

Set 7

party
parties
city
cities
puppy
puppies
curry
curries
hobby
hobbies
worry
worries
story
stories
fairy
fairies

Set 8

life
lives
thief
thieves
scarf
scarves
knife
knives
loaf
loaves
leaf
leaves
sheaf
sheaves
self
selves

Summary

You may wish to photocopy this page and cut it into sets, so that you can give your children a list of the words they will be focusing on each week.

Set 9

mouse
mice
goose
geese
child
children
man
men
woman
women
fungus
fungi
tooth
teeth
fish
sheep

Set 10

use
useful
dread
dreadful
care
careful
cheer
cheerful
skill
skilful
colour
colourful
beauty
beautiful
plenty
plentiful

Set 11

automatic
autopilot
automobile
autobiography
autograph
telepathy
telephone
television
telegraph
telescope
biscuit
bilingual
bicentenary
biceps
binocular
bifocal

Set 12

circle
circumference
circular
circus
circuit
circumnavigate
circumscribe
circumstance
transport
transmit
transparent
transparency
transatlantic
translate
transform
translation

Set 13

electric
electricity
electrician
electrical
mechanic
mechanical
mechanism
mechanise
meteor
meteorite
meteorology
meteoric
prison
prisoner
imprisoned
imprisonment

Set 14

cinema
decide
cereal
centre
cylinder
mercy
celebration
December
circulation
cyclone
circumstances
accident
circuit
circle
certificate
circus

Set 15

scone
score
scale
cough
collar
container
compass
encourage
cabbage
escape
custard
cucumber
cupboard
cobweb
concerned
concentrate

Set 16

flight
freight
eight
height
sprightly
night
slight
straight
thief
niece
piece
field
lie
fiery
fierce
fiesta

Summary

You may wish to photocopy this page and cut it into sets, so that you can give your children a list of the words they will be focusing on each week.

Set 17

earth
heart
fearsome
hearth
beard
smear
search
yearn
four
neighbour
flour
colour
hour
mourn
tour
honourable

Set 18

scene
seen
cereal
serial
where
wear
tear
tier
knight
night
grate
great
key
quay
pane
pain

Set 19

electrician
optician
magician
politician
physician
musician
ration
station
invitation
multiplication
creation
elation
foundation
translation
communication
education

Set 20

reflection
section
correction
direction
attraction
distraction
fiction
faction
sanction
reduction
diction
fraction
collection
construction
infection
traction

Set 21

aggression
session
confession
impression
depression
percussion
mission
passion
possession
dispossession
progression
profession
discussion
oppression
permission
procession

Set 22

mansion
explosion
occasion
conclusion
division
extension
confusion
decision
collision
television
vision
invasion
expansion
revision
exclusion
inclusion

Set 23

dilution
pollution
contribution
distribution
expedition
addition
repetition
position
condition
competition
lotion
potion
promotion
devotion
completion
deletion

Set 24

jewellery
explanatory
voluntary
dictionary
factory
literacy
library
definitely
miserable
literature
interested
desperate
generous
marvellous
Wednesday
familiar

Summary

You may wish to photocopy this page and cut it into sets, so that you can give your children a list of the words they will be focusing on each week.

Set 25

generally
interest
poisonous
secretary
separate
business
boundary
difference
original
company
different
centre
frightening
general
offering
family

Set 26

proper
improper
mature
immature
patient
impatient
polite
impolite
attentive
inattentive
convenient
inconvenient
accurate
inaccurate
active
inactive

Set 27

logical
illogical
legal
illegal
literate
illiterate
legible
illegible
relevant
irrelevant
regular
irregular
removable
irremovable
replaceable
irreplaceable

Set 28

vice
vicious
grace
gracious
space
spacious
precious
conscious
delicious
malice
malicious
suspicious
ambitious
caution
cautious
fictitious

Set 29

official
special
artificial
partial
confidential
essential
initial
financial
commercial
provincial
anxiety
anxious
infect
infectious
infection
nutritious

Set 30

observe
observant
observance
observation
expectant
expectation
hesitate
hesitant
hesitancy
hesitation
tolerate
tolerant
tolerance
toleration
substance
substantial

Set 31

innocent
innocence
innocently
decent
decency
frequent
frequency
confident
confidence
confidential
assistant
assistance
obedient
obedience
independent
independence

Set 32

refer
referring
referred
referral
prefer
preferring
preferred
transfer
transferring
transferred
transference
transferable
reference
referee
preference
preferable

Summary

You may wish to photocopy this page and cut it into sets, so that you can give your children a list of the words they will be focusing on each week.

Set 33

accommodate
accommodation
accompany
accompaniment
according
achieve
aggressive
amateur
ancient
apparent
appreciate
appreciation
attached
attachment
available
availability

Set 34

average
awkward
bargain
bruise
category
cemetery
committee
communicate
communication
community
competition
competitive
conscience
conscious
controversy
controversial

Set 35

convenience
conveniently
correspond
correspondence
critic
critical
criticise
curiosity
curious
definite
definition
desperate
determined
develop
dictionary
disastrous

Set 36

embarrass
environment
equip
equipped
equipment
especially
exaggerate
exaggeration
excellence
excellent
existence
explanation
familiar
foreign
forty
frequently

Set 37

government
guarantee
harass
hindrance
identity
identification
immediate
immediately
individual
interfere
interrupt
language
leisure
lightning
marvellous
mischief

Set 38

mischievous
muscle
necessary
necessarily
neighbour
nuisance
occupy
occupation
occur
opportunity
parliament
persuade
persuasion
physical
prejudice
privilege

Set 39

profession
programme
pronounce
pronunciation
queue
recognise
recognition
recommend
relevant
restaurant
rhyme
rhythm
sacrifice
secretary
shoulder
signature

Set 40

sincere
sincerely
soldier
stomach
sufficient
suggest
symbol
system
systematic
temperature
thorough
twelfth
variety
vegetable
vehicle
yacht